Transforms in CSS

Eric A. Meyer

Beijing · Cambridge · Farnham · Köln · Sebastopol · Tokyo

Transforms in CSS

by Eric A. Meyer

Copyright © 2015 Eric A. Meyer. All rights reserved.

Printed in the United States of America.

Published by O'Reilly Media, Inc., 1005 Gravenstein Highway North, Sebastopol, CA 95472.

O'Reilly books may be purchased for educational, business, or sales promotional use. Online editions are also available for most titles (*http://safaribooksonline.com*). For more information, contact our corporate/institutional sales department: 800-998-9938 or *corporate@oreilly.com*.

Editor: Meg Foley	**Interior Designer:** David Futato
Production Editor: Colleen Lobner	**Cover Designer:** Ellie Volckhausen
Copyeditor: Sonia Saruba	**Illustrator:** Rebecca Demarest
Proofreader: Amanda Kersey	

June 2015: First Edition

Revision History for the First Edition

2015-05-29: First Release

See *http://oreilly.com/catalog/errata.csp?isbn=9781491928158* for release details.

The O'Reilly logo is a registered trademark of O'Reilly Media, Inc. *Transforms in CSS*, the cover image of salmon, and related trade dress are trademarks of O'Reilly Media, Inc.

978-1-491-92815-8

[LSI]

Table of Contents

Preface

Conventions Used in This Book

The following typographical conventions are used in this book:

Italic
> Indicates new terms, URLs, email addresses, filenames, and file extensions.

`Constant width`
> Used for program listings, as well as within paragraphs to refer to program elements such as variable or function names, databases, data types, environment variables, statements, and keywords.

`Constant width bold`
> Shows commands or other text that should be typed literally by the user.

`Constant width italic`
> Shows text that should be replaced with user-supplied values or by values determined by context.

> This element signifies a general note.

> This element indicates a warning or caution.

Using Code Examples

This book is here to help you get your job done. In general, if example code is offered with this book, you may use it in your programs and documentation. You do not need to contact us for permission unless you're reproducing a significant portion of the code. For example, writing a program that uses several chunks of code from this book does not require permission. Selling or distributing a CD-ROM of examples from O'Reilly books does require permission. Answering a question by citing this book and quoting example code does not require permission. Incorporating a significant amount of example code from this book into your product's documentation does require permission.

We appreciate, but do not require, attribution. An attribution usually includes the title, author, publisher, and ISBN. For example: "*Transforms in CSS* by Eric A. Meyer (O'Reilly). Copyright 2015 Eric A. Meyer, 978-1-491-92815-8."

If you feel your use of code examples falls outside fair use or the permission given above, feel free to contact us at *permissions@oreilly.com*.

Safari® Books Online

Safari Books Online is an on-demand digital library that delivers expert content in both book and video form from the world's leading authors in technology and business.

Technology professionals, software developers, web designers, and business and creative professionals use Safari Books Online as their primary resource for research, problem solving, learning, and certification training.

Safari Books Online offers a range of plans and pricing for enterprise, government, education, and individuals.

Members have access to thousands of books, training videos, and prepublication manuscripts in one fully searchable database from publishers like O'Reilly Media, Prentice Hall Professional, Addison-Wesley Professional, Microsoft Press, Sams, Que, Peachpit Press, Focal Press, Cisco Press, John Wiley & Sons, Syngress, Morgan Kaufmann, IBM Redbooks, Packt, Adobe Press, FT Press, Apress, Manning, New Riders, McGraw-Hill, Jones & Bartlett, Course Technology, and hundreds more. For more information about Safari Books Online, please visit us online.

How to Contact Us

Please address comments and questions concerning this book to the publisher:

O'Reilly Media, Inc.
1005 Gravenstein Highway North
Sebastopol, CA 95472
800-998-9938 (in the United States or Canada)
707-829-0515 (international or local)
707-829-0104 (fax)

We have a web page for this book, where we list errata, examples, and any additional information. You can access this page at *http://bit.ly/transforms-in-css*.

To comment or ask technical questions about this book, send email to *bookquestions@oreilly.com*.

For more information about our books, courses, conferences, and news, see our website at *http://www.oreilly.com*.

Find us on Facebook: *http://facebook.com/oreilly*

Follow us on Twitter: *http://twitter.com/oreillymedia*

Watch us on YouTube: *http://www.youtube.com/oreillymedia*

Transforms

Ever since the inception of Cascading Style Sheets (CSS), elements have been rectangular and firmly oriented on the horizontal and vertical axes. A number of tricks arose to make elements look like they were tilted and so on, but underneath it all was a rigid grid. In the late 2000s, an interest grew in being able to break the shackles of that grid and transform objects in interesting ways—and not just in two dimensions.

If you've ever positioned an object, whether relatively or absolutely, then you've already transformed that object. For that matter, any time you used floats or negative-margin tricks (or both), you transformed an object. All of those are examples of *translation*, or the movement of an element from where it would normally appear to some other place. With CSS transforms, you have a new way to translate elements, and a whole lot more. Whether it's as simple as rotating some photographs a bit to make them appear more natural, or creating interfaces where information can be revealed by flipping over elements, or just doing interesting perspective tricks with sidebars, CSS transforms can—if you'll pardon the obvious expression—transform the way you design.

Coordinate Systems

Before embarking on this journey, let's take a moment to orient ourselves. Two types of coordinate systems are used in transforms, and it's a good idea to be familiar with both.

 If you're already well familiar with Cartesian and spherical coordinate systems, particularly as used in computing, feel free to skip to the next section.

The first is the Cartesian coordinate system, or what's often called the x/y/z coordinate system. This system is a way of describing the position of a point in space using two numbers (for two-dimensional placement) or three numbers (for three-dimensional placement). In CSS, the system uses three axes: the x, or horizontal axis; the y, or vertical axis; and the z, or depth axis. This is illustrated in Figure 1.

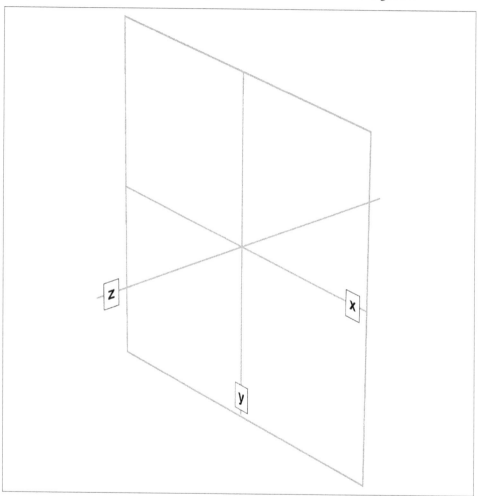

Figure 1. The three Cartesian axes used in CSS transforms

For any 2D (two-dimensional) transform, you only need to worry about the x- and y-axes. By convention, positive x values go to the right, and negative values go to the left. Similarly, positive y values go downward along the y-axis, while negative values go upward along the y-axis.

That might seem a little weird, since we tend to think that higher numbers should place something higher up, not lower down, as many of us learned in pre-algebra. (This why the "y" label is at the bottom of the y-axis in Figure 1: the labels are placed in the positive direction on all three axes.) If you are experienced with absolute positioning in CSS, think of the *top* property values for absolutely positioned elements: they get moved downward for positive *top* values, and upward when *top* has a negative length.

Given this, in order to move an element leftward and down, you would give it a negative x and a positive y value, like this:

```
translateX(-5em) translateY(33px)
```

That is in fact a valid transform value, as we'll see in just a bit. Its effect is to translate (move) the element five ems to the left and 33 pixels down.

If you want to transform something in three-dimensional space, then you add a z-axis value. This axis is the one that "sticks out" of the display and runs straight through your head. In a theoretical sense, that is. Positive z values are closer to you, and negative z values are further away from you. In this regard, it's exactly like the z-index property.

So let's say that we want to take the element we moved before and add a z-axis value:

```
translateX(-5em) translateY(33px) translateZ(200px)
```

Now the element will appear 200 pixels closer to us than it would be without the z value.

Well you might wonder exactly how an element can be moved 200 pixels closer to you, given that holographic displays are regrettably rare and expensive. How many molecules of air between you and your monitor are equivalent to 200 pixels? What does an element moving closer to you even look like, and what happens if it gets *too* close? These are excellent questions that we'll get to later on. For now, just accept that moving an element along the z-axis appears to move it closer or farther away.

The really important thing to remember is that every element carries its own frame of reference and so considers its axes with respect to itself. That is to say, if you rotate an element, the axes rotate along with it, as illustrated in Figure 2. Any further transforms are calculated with respect to those rotated axes, not the axes of the display.

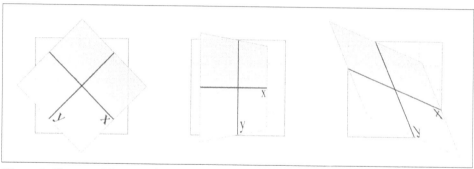

Figure 2. Elemental frames of reference

Speaking of rotations, the other coordinate system used in CSS transforms is a spherical system, which describes angles in 3D space. It's illustrated in Figure 3.

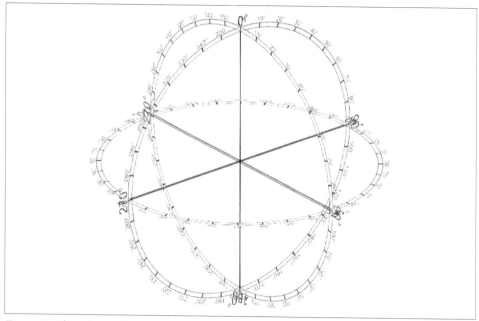

Figure 3. The spherical coordinate system used in CSS transforms

For the purposes of 2D transforms, you only have to worry about a single 360-degree polar system: the one that sits on the plane described by the x- and y-axes. When it comes to rotations, a 2D rotation actually describes a rotation around the z-axis. Similarly, rotations around the x-axis tilt the element toward or away from you, and rotations around the y-axis turn the element from side to side. These are illustrated in Figure 4.

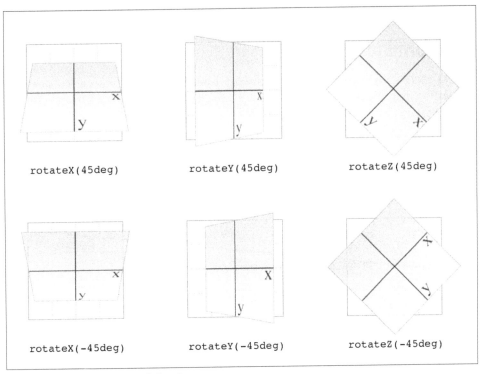

rotateX(45deg) rotateY(45deg) rotateZ(45deg)

rotateX(-45deg) rotateY(-45deg) rotateZ(-45deg)

Figure 4. Rotations around the three axes

But back to 2D rotations. Suppose you wanted to rotate an element 45 degrees clockwise in the plane of the display (i.e., around the z-axis). The transform value you're most likely to use is:

```
rotate(45deg)
```

Change that to –45deg, and the element will rotate counterclockwise (anticlockwise for our international friends) around the z-axis. In other words, it will rotate in the xy plane, as illustrated in Figure 5.

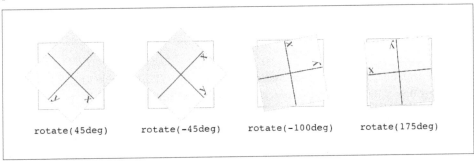

rotate(45deg) rotate(-45deg) rotate(-100deg) rotate(175deg)

Figure 5. Rotations in the xy plane

All right, now that we have our bearings, let's get started with transforms!

Transforming

There's really only one property that applies transforms, along with a few ancillary properties that affect exactly how the transforms are applied. We'll start with the Big Cheese.

<table>
<tr><td colspan="2" align="center">**transform**</td></tr>
<tr><td>**Values:**</td><td>`<transform-list> | none | inherit`</td></tr>
<tr><td>**Initial value:**</td><td>`none`</td></tr>
<tr><td>**Applies to:**</td><td>All elements except "atomic inline-level" boxes (see explanation)</td></tr>
<tr><td>**Inherited:**</td><td>No</td></tr>
<tr><td>**Percentages:**</td><td>Refer to the size of the bounding box (see explanation)</td></tr>
<tr><td>**Computed value:**</td><td>As specified, except for relative length values, which are converted to an absolute length</td></tr>
</table>

First off, let's clear up the matter of the *bounding box*. For any element being affected by CSS, this is the border box; that is, the outermost edge of the element's border. That means that any outlines and margins are ignored for the purposes of calculating the bounding box.

 If a table-display element is being transformed, its bounding box is the table wrapper box, which encloses the table box and any associated caption box.

If you're transforming a Scalable Vector Graphics (SVG) element with CSS, then its bounding box is its SVG-defined *object bounding box*. Simple enough!

Note that all transformed elements (i.e., elements with `transform` set to a value other than none) have their own stacking context. While the scaled element may be much smaller or larger than it was before the transform was applied, the actual space on the page that the element occupies remains the same as before the transform was applied. This is true for all the transform functions.

Now, the value entry `<transform-list>` requires some explanation. This placeholder refers to a list of one or more transform functions, one after the other, in space-separated format. It looks like this, with the result shown in Figure 6:

```
#example {transform: rotate(30deg) skewX(-25deg) scaleY(2);}
```

Figure 6. A transformed div element

The functions are processed one at a time, starting with the first (leftmost) and proceeding to the last (rightmost). This first-to-last processing order is important, because changing the order can lead to drastically different results. Consider the following two rules, which have the results shown in Figure 7:

```
img#one {transform: translateX(200px) rotate(45deg);}
img#two {transform: rotate(45deg) translateX(200px);}
```

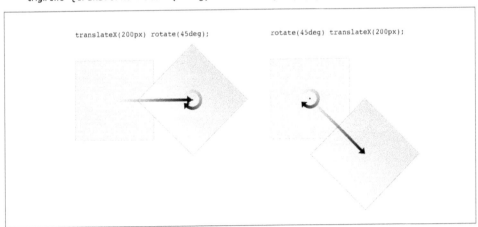

Figure 7. Different transform lists, different results

In the first instance, an image is translated (moved) 200 pixels along its x-axis and then rotated 45 degrees. In the second instance, an image is rotated 45 degrees and then moved 200 pixels along its x-axis—that's the x-axis of the transformed element, *not* of the parent element, page, or viewport. In other words, when an element is rotated, its x-axis (along with its other axes) rotates along with it. All element transforms are conducted with respect to the element's own frame of reference.

Compare this to a situation where an element is translated and then scaled, or vice versa; it doesn't matter which is which, because the end result is the same:

```
img#one {transform: translateX(100px) scale(1.2);}
img#two {transform: scale(1.2) translateX(100px);}
```

The situations where the order doesn't matter are far outnumbered by the situations where it does; so in general, it's a good idea to just assume the order always matters, even when it technically doesn't.

Note that when you have a series of transform functions, all of them must be properly formatted; that is, they must be valid. If even one function is invalid, it renders the entire value invalid. Consider:

```
img#one {transform: translateX(100px) scale(1.2) rotate(22);}
```

Because the value for `rotate()` is invalid—rotational values must have a unit—the entire value is dropped. The image in question will simply sit there in its initial untransformed state, neither translated nor scaled, let alone rotated.

It's also the case that transforms are not usually cumulative. That is to say, if you apply a transform to an element and then later want to add a transformation, you need to restate the original transform. Consider the following scenarios, illustrated in Figure 8:

```
#ex01 {transform: rotate(30deg) skewX(-25deg);}
#ex01 {transform: scaleY(2);}
#ex02 {transform: rotate(30deg) skewX(-25deg);}
#ex02 {transform: rotate(30deg) skewX(-25deg) scaleY(2);}
```

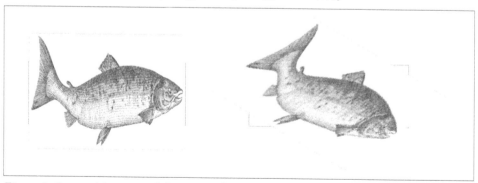

Figure 8. Overwriting or modifying transforms

In the first case, the second rule completely replaces the first, meaning that the element is only scaled along the y-axis. This actually makes some sense; it's the same as if you declare a font size and then elsewhere declare a different font size for the same element. You don't get a cumulative font size that way. You just get one size or the other. In the second example, the entirety of the first set of transforms is included in the second set, so they all are applied along with the `scaleY()` function.

There is an exception to this, which is that animated transforms, whether using transitions or actual animations, *are* additive. That way, you can take an element that's transformed and then animate one of its transform functions without overwriting the others. For example, assume you had:

```
img#one {transform: translateX(100px) scale(1.2);}
```

If you then animate the element's rotation angle, it will rotate from its translated, scaled state to the new angle, and its translation and scale will remain in place.

What makes this interesting is that even if you don't explicitly specify a transition or animation, you can still create additive transforms via the user-interaction pseudoclasses, such as `:hover`. That's because things like hover effects are types of transitions; they're just not invoked using the transition properties. Thus, you could declare:

```
img#one {transform: translateX(100px) scale(1.2);}
img#one:hover {transform: rotate(-45deg);}
```

This would rotate the translated, scaled image 45 degrees to its left on hover. The rotation would take place over zero seconds because no transition interval was declared, but it's still an implicit transition. Thus, any state change can be thought of as a transition, and thus any transforms that are applied as a result of those state changes are additive with previous transforms.

There's one important caveat: as of this writing, transforms are not applied to "atomic inline-level" boxes. These are inline boxes like spans, hyperlinks, and so on. Those elements can be transformed if their block-level parent is transformed, in which case they go along for the ride. But you can't just rotate a `span` unless you've changed its display role via `display: block`, `display: inline-block`, or something along those lines. The reason for this limitation boils down to an uncertainty. Suppose you have a `span` (or any inline-level box) that breaks across multiple lines. If you rotate it, what happens? Does each line box rotate with respect to itself, or should all the line boxes be rotated as a single group? There's no clear answer, and the debate continues, so for now you can't directly transform inline-level boxes.

 As of late 2014, `transform` and its associated properties still had to be vendor-prefixed in WebKit and Blink browsers like Safari and Chrome. No prefixes were needed in other major user agents. This restriction was finally dropped in early 2015.

The Transform Functions

There are, as of this writing, 21 different transform functions, employing a number of different value patterns to get their jobs done. Table 1 provides a list of all the available transform functions, minus their value patterns.

Table 1. Transform functions

translate()	scale()	rotate()	skew()	matrix()
translate3d()	scale3d()	rotate3d()	skewX()	matrix3d()
translateX()	scaleX()	rotateX()	skewY()	perspective()
translateY()	scaleY()	rotateY()		
translateZ()	scaleZ()	rotateZ()		

As previously stated, the most common value pattern for `transform` is a space-separated list of one or more functions, processed from first (leftmost) to last (rightmost), and all of the functions must have valid values. If any one of the functions is invalid, it will invalidate the entire value of `transform`, thus preventing any transformation at all.

Translation functions

A translation transform is just a move along one or more axes. For example, `translateX()` moves an element along its own x-axis, `translateY()` moves it along its y-axis, and `translateZ()` moves it along its z-axis.

Functions	Permitted values
translateX(), translateY()	*<length>*	*<percentage>*

These are usually referred to as the "2D" translation functions, since they can slide an element up and down, or side to side, but not forward or backward along the z-axis. Each of these functions accepts a single distance value, expressed as either a length or a percentage.

If the value is a length, then the effect is about what you'd expect. Translate an element 200 pixels along the x-axis with `translateX(200px)`, and it will move 200 pixels to its right. Change that to `translateX(-200px)`, and it will move 200 pixels to its left. For `translateY()`, positive values move the element downward, while negative values move it upward, both with respect to the element itself. Thus, if you flip the element upside down by rotation, positive `translateY()` values will actually move the element downward on the page.

If the value is a percentage, then the distance is calculated as a percentage of the element's own size. Thus, translateX(50%) will move an element 300 pixels wide and 200 pixels tall to its right by 150 pixels, and translateY(-10%) will move that same element upward (with respect to itself) by 20 pixels.

Function	Permitted values
translate()	[<length> | <percentage>] [, <length> | <percentage>]?

If you want to translate an element along both the x- and y-axes at the same time, then translate() makes it simple. Just supply the x value first and the y value second, and it will act the same as if you combined translateX() translateY(). If you omit the y value, then it's assumed to be zero. Thus, translate(2em) is treated as if it were translate(2em,0), which is also the same as translateX(2em). See Figure 9 for some examples of 2D translation.

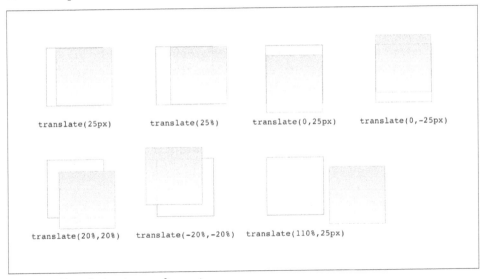

Figure 9. Translating in two dimensions

According to the latest version of the specification, both of the 2D translation functions can be given a unitless number. In this case, the number is treated as being expressed in terms of a "user unit," which is treated the same as a pixel unless otherwise defined. The CSS specification does not explain how a user unit is otherwise defined; however, the SVG specification does, albeit briefly. In the field, no browser tested as of this writing supported unitless numbers of translation values, so the capability is academic, at best.

Function	Permitted value
translateZ()	<length>

This function translates elements along the z-axis, thus moving them into the third dimension. Unlike the 2D translation functions, translateZ() only accepts length values. Percentage values are *not* permitted for translateZ(), or indeed for any z-axis value.

Functions	Permitted values
translate3d()	[<length> | <percentage>], [<length> | <percentage>], [<length>]

Much like translate() does for x and y translations, translate3d() is a shorthand function that incorporates the x, y, and z translation values into a single function. This is obviously handy if you want to move an element over, up, and forward in one fell swoop. See Figure 10 for an illustration of how 3D translation works. There, each arrow represents the translation along that axis, arriving at a point in 3D space. The dashed lines show the distance and direction from the origin point (the intersection of the three axes) and the distance above the xz plane.

Unlike translate(), there is no fallback for situations where translate3d() does not contain three values. Thus, translate3d(1em,-50px) should be treated as invalid by user agents instead of being assumed to be translate3d(2em,-50px,0).

Scale functions

A scale transform makes an element larger or smaller, depending on what value you use. These values are unitless real numbers and are always positive. On the 2D plane, you can scale along the x- and y-axes individually, or scale them together.

Functions	Permitted value
scaleX(), scaleY(), scaleZ()	<number>

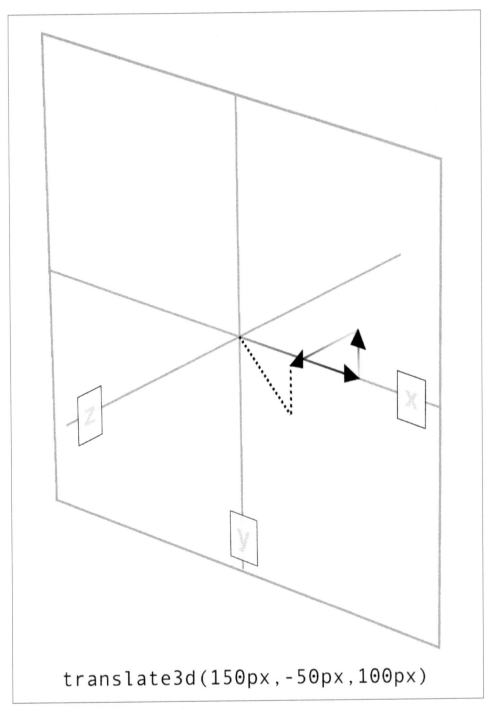

`translate3d(150px,-50px,100px)`

Figure 10. Translating in three dimensions

The number value supplied to a scale function is a multiplier; thus, scaleX(2) will make an element twice as wide as it was before the transformation, whereas scaleY(0.5) will make it half as tall. Given this, you might expect that percentage values are permissible as scaling values, but they aren't.

Function	Permitted value
scale()	<number>[, <number>]?

If you want to scale along both axes simultaneously, use scale(). The x value is always first and the y always second, so scale(2,0.5) will make the element twice as wide and half as tall as it was before being transformed. If you only supply one number, it is used as the scaling value for both axes; thus, scale(2) will make the element twice as wide *and* twice as tall. This is in contrast to translate(), where an omitted second value is always set to zero. scale(1) will scale an element to be exactly the same size it was before you scaled it, as will scale(1,1). Just in case you were dying to do that.

Figure 11 shows a few examples of element scaling, using both the single-axis scaling functions, as well as the combined scale().

Figure 11. Scaled elements

Of course, if you can scale in two dimensions, you can also scale in three. CSS offers scaleZ() for scaling just along the z-axis, and scale3d() for scaling along all three axes at once. These really only have an effect if the element has any depth, which elements don't by default. If you do make a change that conveys depth—say, rotating an element around the x- or y-axes—then there is a depth that can be scaled, and either scaleZ() or scale3d() can do so.

Function	Permitted value
scale3d()	*<number>, <number>, <number>*

Similar to translate3d(), scale3d() requires all three numbers to be valid. If you fail to do this, then the malformed scale3d() will invalidate the entire transform value to which it belongs.

Rotation functions

A rotation function causes an element to be rotated around an axis, or around an arbitrary vector in 3D space. There are four simple rotation functions, and one less-simple function meant specifically for 3D.

Functions	Permitted values
rotate(), rotateX(), rotateY(), rotateZ()	*<angle>*

All four basic rotation functions accept just one value: a degree. This can be expressed using any of the valid degree units (deg, grad, rad, and turn) and a number, either positive or negative. If a value's number runs outside the usual range for the given unit, it will be normalized to fit into the accepted range. In other words, a value of 437deg will be tilted the same as if it were 77deg, or, for that matter, -283deg.

Note, however, that these are only exactly equivalent if you don't animate the rotation in some fashion. That is to say, animating a rotation of 1100deg will spin the element around several times before coming to rest at a tilt of -20 degrees (or 340 degrees, if you like). By contrast, animating a rotation of -20deg will tilt the element a bit to the left, with no spinning; and of course animating a rotation of 340deg will animate an almost-full spin to the right. All three animations come to the same end state, but the process of getting there is very different in each case.

The function rotate() is a straight 2D rotation, and the one you're most likely to use. It is equivalent to rotateZ() because it rotates the element around the z-axis (the one that shoots straight out of your display and through your eyeballs). In a similar manner, rotateX() causes rotation around the x-axis, thus causing the element to tilt toward or away from you; and rotateY() rotates the element around its y-axis, as though it were a door. These are all illustrated in Figure 12.

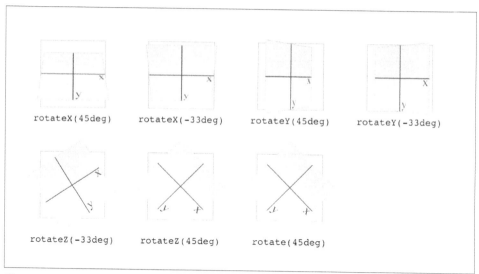

Figure 12. Rotations around the three axes

 Several of the examples in Figure 12 present a fully 3D appearance. This is only possible with certain values of the properties `transform-style` and `perspective`, described in a later section and omitted here for clarity. This will be true throughout this text in any situation where 3D-transformed elements appear to be fully three-dimensional. This is important to keep in mind because if you just try to apply the transform functions shown, you won't get the same visual results as in the figures.

Function	Permitted value
rotate3d()	*<number>, <number>, <number>, <angle>*

If you're comfortable with vectors and want to rotate an element through 3D space, then `rotate3d()` is for you. The first three numbers specify the x, y, and z components of a vector in 3D space, and the degree value (angle) determines the amount of rotation around the declared 3D vector.

To start with a simple example, the 3D equivalent to `rotate(45deg)` is `rotate3d(0,0,1,45deg)`. This specifies a vector of zero magnitude on the x- and y-axes, and a magnitude of 1 along the z-axis. In other words, it describes the z-axis. The element is thus rotated 45 degrees around that vector, as shown in Figure 13. This figure also shows the appropriate `rotate3d()` values to rotate an element by 45 degrees around the x- and y-axes.

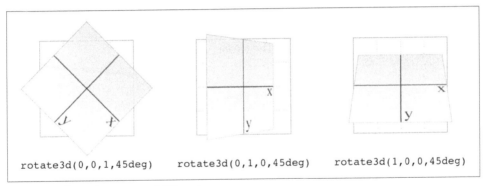

rotate3d(0,0,1,45deg)   rotate3d(0,1,0,45deg)   rotate3d(1,0,0,45deg)

Figure 13. Rotations around 3D vectors

A little more complicated is something like `rotate3d(-0.95,0.5,1,45deg)`, where the described vector points off into 3D space between the axes. In order to understand how this works, let's start with a simple example: `rotateZ(45deg)` (illustrated in Figure 13). The equivalent is `rotate3d(0,0,1,45deg)`. The first three numbers describe the components of a vector that has no x or y magnitude, and a z magnitude of 1. Thus, it points along the z-axis in a positive direction; that is, toward the viewer. The element is then rotated clockwise as you look toward the origin of the vector. Simple enough.

Similarly, the 3D equivalent of `rotateX(45deg)` is `rotate3d(1,0,0,45deg)`. The vector points along the x-axis in the positive direction (to the right). If you stand at the end of that vector and look toward its origin, then you rotate the element 45 degrees clockwise around the vector. Thus, from the usual viewer placement, the top of the element rotates away from and the bottom rotates toward the viewer.

Let's make it slightly more complex: suppose you have `rotate3d(1,1,0,45deg)`. When viewed on your monitor, that describes a vector running from the top-left to bottom-right corner, going right through the center of the element (by default, anyway; we'll see how to change that later on). So the element's rectangle has a line running through it at a 45-degree angle, effectively spearing it. Then the vector rotates 45 degrees, taking the element with it. The rotation is clockwise as you look back toward the vector's origin, so again, the top of the element rotates away from the viewer, while the bottom rotates toward the viewer. If we were to change the rotation to `rotate3d(1,1,0,90deg)`, then the element would be edge-on to the viewer, tilted at a 45-degree angle and facing off toward the upper right. Try it with a piece of paper: draw a line from the top left to bottom right, and then rotate the paper around that line.

Okay, so given all that, try visualizing how the vector is determined for `rotate3d(-0.95,0.5,1,45deg)`. If we assume a cube 200 pixels on a side, the vector's components are 190 pixels to the *left* along the x-axis, 100 pixels down along the y-axis, and 200 pixels toward the views along the z-axis. The vector goes from the origin point (0, 0, 0) to the point (-190px, 100px, 200px). Figure 14 depicts that vector, as well as the final result presented to the viewer.

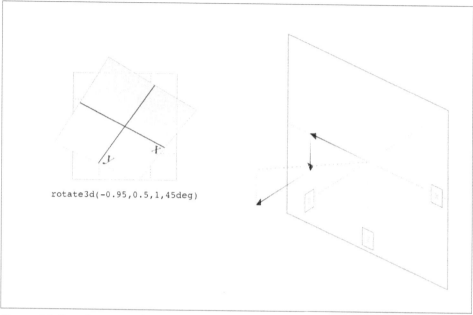

Figure 14. Rotation around a 3D vector, and how that vector is determined

So the vector is like a metal rod speared through the element being rotated. As we look back along the line of the vector, the rotation is 45 degrees clockwise. But since the vector points left, down, and forward, that means the top left corner of the element rotates toward the viewer, and the bottom right rotates away, as shown in Figure 14.

Just to be crystal clear, `rotate3d(1,1,0,45deg)` is *not* equivalent to `rotateX(45deg)` `rotateY(45deg)` `rotateZ(0deg)`! It's an easy mistake to make, and many people—including several online tutorial authors and, until researching and writing this section, your humble correspondent—have made it. It seems like it should be equivalent, but it really isn't. If we place that vector inside the imaginary 200 × 200 × 200 cube previously mentioned, the axis of rotation would go from the origin point to a point 200 pixels right and 200 pixels down (200, 200, 0).

Having done that, the axis of rotation is shooting through the element from the top left to the bottom right, at a 45-degree angle. The element then rotates 45 degrees clockwise around that diagonal, as you look back toward its origin (the top left), which rotates the top-right corner of the element away and a bit to the left, while the bottom-left corner rotates closer and a bit to the right. This is distinctly different than the result of `rotateX(45deg) rotateY(45deg) rotateZ(0deg)`, as you can see in Figure 15.

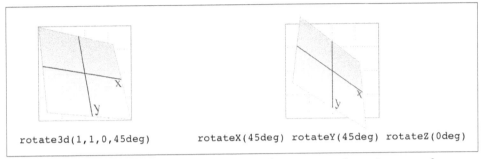

`rotate3d(1,1,0,45deg)`   `rotateX(45deg) rotateY(45deg) rotateZ(0deg)`

Figure 15. The difference between rotating around two axes and rotating around a 3D axis

Skew functions

When you skew an element, you slant it along one or both of the x- and y-axes. There is no z-axis or other 3D skewing.

Functions	Permitted value
skewX(), skewY()	*<angle>*

In both cases, you supply an angle value, and the element is skewed to match that angle. It's much easier to show skewing rather than try to explain it in words, so Figure 16 shows a number of skew examples along the x- and y-axes.

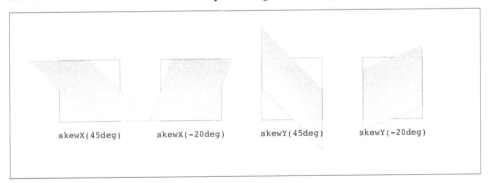

`skewX(45deg)`   `skewX(-20deg)`   `skewY(45deg)`   `skewY(-20deg)`

Figure 16. Skewing along the x- and y-axes

Function	Permitted values
skew()	*<angle>* [, *<angle>*]?

The behavior of including `skew(a,b)` is different from including `skewX(a)` with `skewY(b)`. Instead, it specifies a 2D skew using the matrix operation `[ax,ay]`. Figure 17 shows some examples of this matrix skewing and how they differ from double-skew transforms that look the same at first, but aren't.

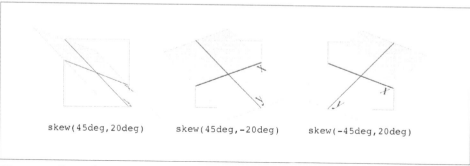

Figure 17. Skewed elements

If you supply two values, the x skew angle is always first, and the y skew angle comes second. If you leave out a y skew angle, then it's treated as zero.

The perspective function

If you're transforming an element in 3D space, you most likely want it to have some perspective. Perspective gives the appearance of front-to-back depth, and you can vary the amount of perspective applied to an element.

Function	Permitted values
perspective()	*<length>*

It might seem a bit weird that you specify perspective as a distance. After all, `perspective(200px)` seems a bit odd when you can't really measure pixels along the z-axis. And yet, here we are. You supply a length, and the illusion of depth is constructed around that value. Lower numbers create more extreme perspective, as though you are right up close to the element and viewing it through a fish-eye lens. Higher numbers create a gentler perspective, as though viewing the element through a zoom lens from far away. *Really* high perspective values create an isometric effect.

This makes a certain amount of sense. If you visualize perspective as a pyramid, with its apex point at the perspective origin and its base the closest thing to you, then a shorter distance between apex and base will create a shallower pyramid, and thus a more extreme distortion. This is illustrated in Figure 18, with hypothetical pyramids representing 200 px, 800 px, and 2,000 px perspective distances.

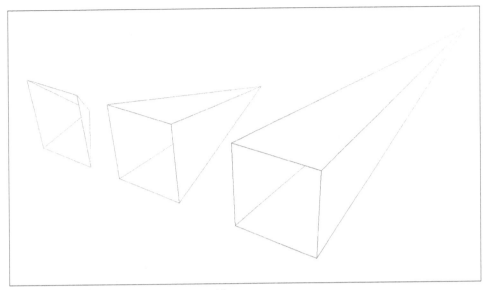

Figure 18. Different perspective pyramids

In the documentation for Safari, Apple writes that perspective values below 300px tend to be extremely distorted, values above 2000px create "very mild" distortion, and values between 500px and 1000px create "moderate perspective." To illustrate this, Figure 19 shows a series of elements with the exact same rotation as displayed with varying perspective values.

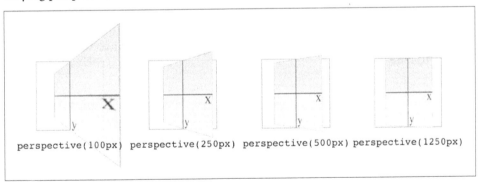

Figure 19. The effects of varying perspective values

Perspective values must always be positive, nonzero lengths. Any other value will cause the perspective() function to be ignored. Also note that its placement in the list of functions is very important. If you look at the code for Figure 19, the perspective() function comes before the rotateY() function. If you were to reverse the order, the rotation would happen before the perspective is applied, so all four examples in Figure 19 would look exactly the same. So if you plan to apply a perspective value via the list of transform functions, make sure it comes first, or at the very least before any transforms that depend on it. This serves as a particularly stark reminder that the order in which you write transform functions can be very important.

 Note that the function perspective() is very similar to the property perspective, which will be covered later, but they are applied in critically different ways. Generally, you will want to use the perspective property instead of the perspective() function, but there may be exceptions.

Matrix functions

If you're a particular fan of advanced math, or stale jokes derived from Wachowski Brothers movies, then these functions will be your favorites.

Function	Permitted values
matrix()	*<number>* [, *<number>*]{5,5}

In the CSS transforms specification, we find the trenchant description of matrix() as a function that "specifies a 2D transformation in the form of a transformation matrix of the six values *a-f*."

First things first: a valid matrix() value is a list of six comma-separated numbers. No more, no less. The values can be positive or negative. Second, the value describes the final transformed state of the element, combining all of the other transform types (rotation, skewing, and so on) into a very compact syntax. Third, very few people actually use this syntax.

We're not actually going to go through the complicated process of actually doing the matrix math. For most readers, it would be an eye-watering wall of apparent gibberish; and for the rest, it would be time wasted on familiar territory. You can certainly research the intricacies of matrix calculations online, and I encourage anyone with an interest to do so. We'll just look at the basics of syntax and usage in CSS.

Here's a brief rundown of how it works. Say you have this function applied to an element:

```
matrix(0.838671, 0.544639, -0.692519, 0.742636, 6.51212, 34.0381)
```

That's the CSS syntax used to describe this transformation matrix:

```
0.838671      -0.692519    0    6.51212
0.544639       0.742636    0    34.0381
0              0           1    0
0              0           0    1
```

Right. So what does that do? It has the result shown in Figure 20, which is exactly the same result as writing this:

```
rotate(33deg) translate(24px,25px) skewX(-10deg)
```

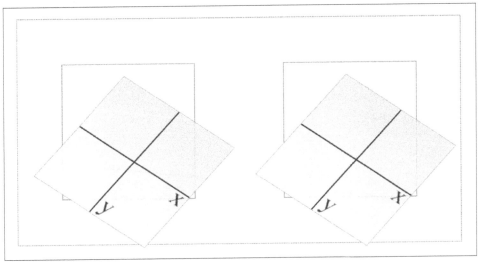

Figure 20. A matrix-transformed element and its functional equivalent

What this comes down to is that if you're familiar with or need to make use of matrix calculations, you can and should absolutely use them. If not, you can chain much more human-readable transform functions together and get the element to the same end state.

Now, that was for plain old 2D transforms. What if you want to use a matrix to transform through three dimensions?

Function	Permitted values
matrix3d()	*<number>* [, *<number>*]{15,15}

Again, just for kicks, we'll savor the definition of `matrix3d()` from the CSS Transforms specification: "specifies a 3D transformation as a 4 × 4 homogeneous matrix of 16 values in column-major order." This means the value of `matrix3d` *must* be a list of 16 comma-separated numbers, no more or less. Those numbers are arranged in a 4 × 4 grid in column order, so the first column of the matrix is formed by the first set of four numbers in the value, the second column by the second set of four numbers, the third column by the third set, and so on. Thus, you can take the following function:

```
matrix3d(
    0.838671, 0, -0.544639, 0.00108928,
    -0.14788, 1, 0.0960346, -0.000192069,
```

```
0.544639, 0, 0.838671, -0.00167734,
20.1281, 25, -13.0713, 1.02614)
```

And write it out as this matrix:

```
0.838671    -0.14788        0.544639     20.1281
0            1              0            25
-0.544639    0.0960346       0.838671    -13.0713
0.00108928  -0.000192069    -0.00167734   1.02614
```

Both of which have an end state equivalent to:

```
perspective(500px) rotateY(33deg) translate(24px,25px) skewX(-10deg)
```

as shown in Figure 21.

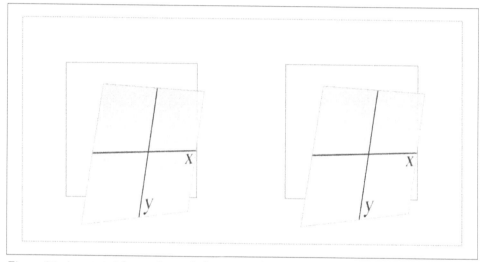

Figure 21. A matrix3d-transformed element and its functional equivalent

A note on end-state equivalence

It's important to keep in mind that only the end states of a matrix() function, and of an equivalent chain of transform functions, can be considered identical. This is for the same reason discussed in the section on rotation: because a rotation angle of 393deg will end with the same visible rotation as an angle of 33deg. This matters if you are animating the transformation, since the former will cause the element to do a barrel roll in the animation, whereas the latter will not. The matrix() version of this end state won't include the barrel roll, either. Instead, it will always use the shortest possible rotation to reach the end state.

To illustrate what this means, consider the following: a transform chain and its matrix() equivalent:

```
    rotate(200deg) translate(24px,25px) skewX(-10deg)
    matrix(-0.939693, -0.34202, 0.507713, -0.879385, -14.0021, -31.7008)
```

Note the rotation of 200 degrees. We naturally interpret this to mean a clockwise rotation of 200 degrees, which it does. If these two transforms are animated, however, they will have act differently: the chained-functions version will indeed rotate 200 degrees clockwise, whereas the `matrix()` version will rotate 160 degrees counter-clockwise. Both will end up in the same place, but will get there in different ways.

There are similar differences that arise even when you might think they wouldn't. Once again, this is because a `matrix()` transformation will always take the shortest possible route to the end state, whereas a transform chain might not. (In fact, it probably doesn't.) Consider these apparently equivalent transforms:

```
    rotate(160deg) translate(24px,25px) rotate(-30deg) translate(-100px)
    matrix(-0.642788, 0.766044, -0.766044, -0.642788, 33.1756, -91.8883)
```

As ever, they end up in the same place. When animated, though, the elements will take different paths to reach that end state. They might not be obviously different at first glance, but the difference is still there.

Of course, none of this matters if you aren't animating the transformation, but it's an important distinction to make nevertheless, because you never know when you'll decide to start animating things. (Hopefully after reading the companion text on animations!)

More Transform Properties

In addition to the base `transform` property, there are a few related properties that help to define things such as the origin point of a transform, the perspective used for a "scene," and more.

Moving the Origin

So far, all of the transforms we've seen have shared one thing in common: the precise center of the element was used as the *transform origin*. For example, when rotating the element, it rotated around its center, instead of, say, a corner. This is the default behavior, but with the property `transform-origin`, you can change it.

Values:	`[ left | center | right | top | bottom | `*`<percentage>`*` | `*`<length>`*` ]`
	 `|`
	   `[ left | center | right | `*`<percentage>`*` | `*`<length>`*` ]`
	   `[ top | center | bottom | `*`<percentage>`*` | `*`<length>`*` ] `*`<length>`*`?`
	 `|`

Initial value:	`50% 50%`
Applies to:	Any transformable element
Inherited:	No
Percentages:	Refer to the size of the bounding box (see explanation)
Computed value:	A percentage, except for length values, which are converted to an absolute length

The syntax definition looks really abstruse and confusing, but it's actually very simple in practice. With `transform-origin`, you supply two or three keywords to define the point around which transforms should be made: first the horizontal, then the vertical, and optionally a length along the z-axis. For the horiztonal and vertical axes, you can use plain-English keywords like `top` and `right`, percentages, lengths, or a combination of different keyword types. For the z-axis, you can't use plain-English keywords or percentages, but can use any length value. Pixels are by far the most common.

Length values are taken as a distance starting from the top-left corner of the element. Thus, `transform-origin: 5em 22px` will place the transform origin 5 em to the right of the left side of the element, and 22 pixels down from the top of the element. Similarly, `transform-origin: 5em 22px -200px` will place it 5 em over, 22 pixels down, and 200 pixels away; that is, 200 pixels behind the place where the element sits.

Percentages are calculated with respect to the corresponding axis and size of the element, as offsets from the element's top-left corner. For example, `transform-origin: 67% 40%` will place the transform origin 67 percent of the width to the right of the element's left side, and 40 percent of the element's height down from the element's top side. Figure 22 illustrates a few origin calculations.

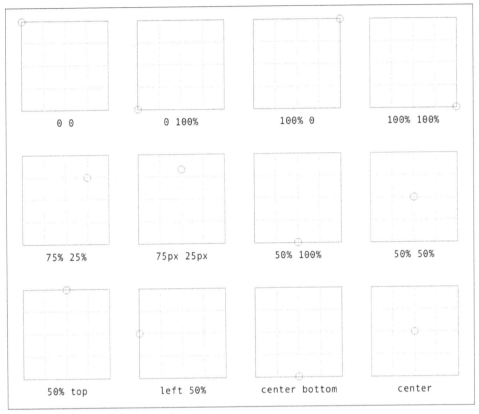

Figure 22. Various origin calculations

All right, so if you change the origin, what happens? The easiest way to visualize this is with 2D rotations. Suppose you rotate an element 45 degrees to the right. Its final placement will depend on its origin. Figure 23 illustrates the the effects of several different transform origins; in each case, the transform origin is marked with a circle.

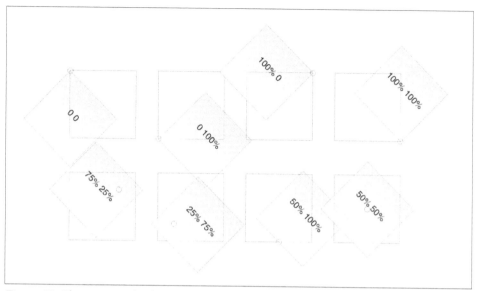

Figure 23. The rotational effects of using various transform origins

The origin matters for other transform types, such as skews and scales. Scaling an element with its origin in the center will pull in all sides equally, whereas scaling an element with a bottom-right origin will cause it to shrink toward that corner. Similarly, skewing an element with respect to its center will result in the same shape as if it's skewed with respect to the top-right corner, but the placement of the shape will be different. Some examples are shown in Figure 24; again, each transform origin is marked with a circle.

The one transform type that isn't really affected by changing the transform origin is translation. If you push an element around with `translate()`, or its cousins like `translateX()` and `translateY()`, it's going to end up in the same place regardless of where the transform origin is located. If that's all the transforming you plan to do, then setting the transform origin is irrelevant. If you ever do anything besides translating, though, the origin will matter. Use it wisely.

Figure 24. The skew effects of using various transform origins

Choosing a 3D Style

If you're setting elements to be transformed through three dimensions—using, say, `translate3d()` or `rotateY()`—you probably expect that the elements will be presented as though they're in a 3D space. And yet, this is not the default behavior. By default, everything looks flat no matter what you do. Fortunately, this can be overridden with the `transform-style` property.

transform-style	
Values:	`flat` | `preserve-3d`
Initial value:	`flat`
Applies to:	Any transformable element
Inherited:	No
Computed value:	As specified

Suppose you have an element you want to move "closer to" your eye, and then tilt away a bit, with a moderate amount of perspective. Something like this rule, as applied to the following HTML:

```
div#inner {transform: perspective(750px) translateZ(60px) rotateX(45deg);}

<div id="outer">
outer
<div id="inner">inner</div>
</div>
```

So you do that, and get the result shown in Figure 25; more or less what you might have expected.

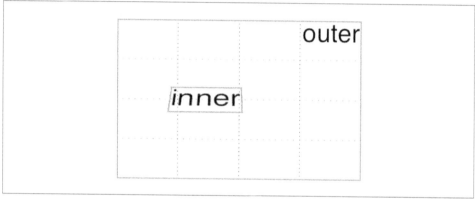

Figure 25. A 3D-transformed inner div

But then you decide to rotate the outer div to one side, and suddenly nothing makes sense any more. The inner div isn't where you envisioned it. In fact, it just looks like a picture pasted to the front of the outer div.

Well, that's exactly what it is, because the default value of transform-style is flat. The inner div got drawn in its moved-forward-tilted-back state, and that was applied to the front of the outer div as if it was an image. So when you rotated the outer div, the flat picture rotated right along with it, as shown in Figure 26:

```
div#outer {transform: perspective(750px) rotateY(60deg) rotateX(-20deg);}
div#inner {transform: perspective(750px) translateZ(60px) rotateX(45deg);}
```

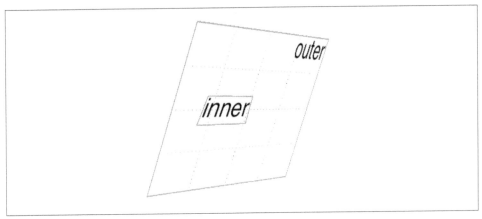

Figure 26. The effects of a flat transform style

Change the value to `preserve-3d`, however, and things are suddenly different. The inner `div` will be drawn as a full 3D object with respect to its parent outer `div`, floating in space nearby, and *not* as a picture pasted on the front of the outer `div`. You can see the results of this change in Figure 27:

```
div#outer {transform: perspective(750px) rotateY(60deg) rotateX(-20deg);
    transform-style: preserve-3d;}
div#inner {transform: perspective(750px) translateZ(60px) rotateX(45deg);}
```

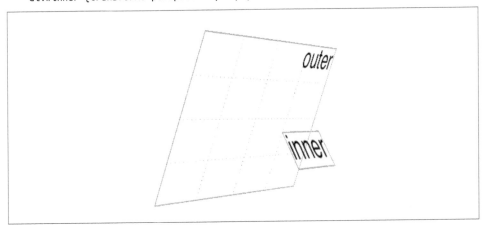

Figure 27. The effects of a 3D-preserved transform style

One important aspect of `transform-style` is that it can be overridden by other properties. The reason is that some values of these other properties require a flattened presentation of an element and its children in order to work at all. In such cases, the value of `transform-style` is forced to be `flat`, regardless of what you may have declared.

So, in order to avoid this overriding behavior, make sure the following properties are set to the listed values:

- `overflow: visible`
- `filter: none`
- `clip: auto`
- `clip-path: none`
- `mask-image: none`
- `mask-border-source: none`
- `mix-blend-mode: normal`

Those are all the default values for those properties, so as long as you don't try to change any of them for your preserved 3D elements, you're fine! But if you find that editing some CSS suddenly flattens out your lovely 3D transforms, one of these properties might be the culprit.

One more note: in addition to the values just mentioned, the value of the property `isolation` must be, or be computed to be, `isolate`. (`isolation` is a compositing property, in case you were wondering.)

Changing Perspective

There are actually two properties that are used to define how perspective is handled: one to define the perspective distance, as with the `perspective()` function discussed in an earlier section; and another to define the perspective's origin point.

Defining a group perspective

First, let's consider the property `perspective`, which accepts a length that defines the depth of the perspective pyramid. At first glance, it looks just like the `perspective()` function discussed earlier, but there are some very critical differences.

perspective

Values: none | *<length>*

Initial value: flat

Applies to: Any transformable element

Inherited: No

Computed value: The absolute length, or else none

As a quick example, if you want to create a very deep perspective, one mimicking the results you'd get from a zoom lens, you might declare something like `perspective: 2500px`. For a shallow depth, one that mimics a closeup fish-eye lens effect, you might declare `perspective: 200px`.

So how does this differ from the `perspective()` function? When you use `perspective()`, you're defining the perspective effect for the element that is given that function. So if you say `transform: perspective(800px) rotateY(-50grad);`, you're applying that perspective to each element that has the rule applied.

With the `perspective` property, on the other hand, you're creating a perspective depth that is applied to all the child elements of the element that received the property. Confused yet? Don't be. Here's a simple illustration of the difference, as shown in Figure 28:

```
div {transform-style: preserve-3d; border: 1px solid gray; width: 660px;}
img {margin: 10px;}
#one {perspective: none;}
#one img {transform: perspective(800px) rotateX(-50grad);}
#two {perspective: 800px;}
#two img {transform: rotateX(-50grad);}

<div><img src="rsq.gif"><img src="rsq.gif"><img src="rsq.gif"></div>
<div id="one"><img src="rsq.gif"><img src="rsq.gif"><img src="rsq.gif"></div>
<div id="two"><img src="rsq.gif"><img src="rsq.gif"><img src="rsq.gif"></div>
```

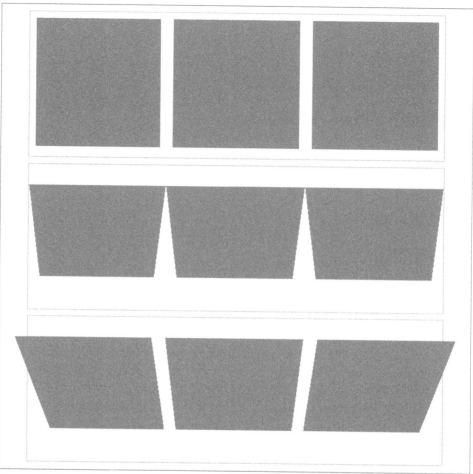

Figure 28. Shared perspective versus individual perspectives

In Figure 28, we first see a line of images that haven't been transformed. In the second line, each image has been rotated 50 gradians (equivalent to 45 degrees) toward us, but each one within its own individual perspective.

In the third line of images, none of them has an individual perspective. Instead, they are all drawn within the perspective defined by `perspective: 800px;` that's been set on the `div` that contains them. Since they all operate within a shared perspective, they look "correct"; that is, like we would expect if we had three physical pictures mounted on a clear sheet of glass and rotated toward us around the center horizontal axis of that glass.

Note that presence of `transform-style: preserve-3d` makes this effect possible, as discussed in the previous section.

This is the critical difference between `perspective`, the property; and `perspective()`, the function. The former creates a 3D space shared by all its children. The latter affects only the element to which it's applied. A less important difference is that the `perspective()` function has to come first or early in its chain of transforms in order to apply to the element as it's transformed through 3D space. The `perspective` property, on the other hand, is applied to all children regardless of where their transforms are declared.

In most cases, you're going to use the `perspective` property instead of the `perspective()` function. In fact, container `div`s (or other elements) are a very common feature of 3D transforms—the way they used to be for page layout—largely to establish a shared perspective. In the previous example, the `<div id="two">` was there solely to serve as a perspective container, so to speak. On the other hand, we couldn't have done what we did without it.

Moving the perspective's origin

When transforming elements in three dimensions—assuming you've allowed them to appear three-dimensional, that is—a perspective will be used. (See `transform-style` and `perspective`, respectively, in previous sections.) That perspective will have an origin, which is also known as the *vanishing point*, and you can change where it's located with the property `perspective-origin`.

perspective-origin

Values:	[left | center | right | top | bottom | <percentage> | <length>]
	|
	  [left | center | right | <percentage> | <length>]
	  [top | center | bottom | <percentage> | <length>] <length>?
	|
	  [center | [left | right]] && [center | [top | bottom]]

Initial value:	50% 50%
Applies to:	Any transformable element
Inherited:	No
Percentages:	Refer to the size of the bounding box (see explanation)
Computed value:	A percentage, except for length values, which are converted to an absolute length

As you've no doubt spotted, `perspective-origin` and `transform-origin` (discussed earlier) have the same value syntax, right down to allowing an optional length value defining an offset along the z-axis. While the way the values are expressed is identical, the effects they have are very different. With `transform-origin`, you define the point around which transforms happen. With `perspective-origin`, you define the point on which sight lines converge.

As with most 3D transform properties, this is more easily demonstrated than described. Consider the following CSS and markup, illustrated in Figure 29:

```
#container {perspective: 850px; perspective-origin: 50% 0%;}
#ruler {height: 50px; background: #DED url(tick.gif) repeat-x;
    transform: rotateX(60deg);
    transform-origin: 50% 100%;}

<div id="container">
    <div id="ruler"></div>
</div>
```

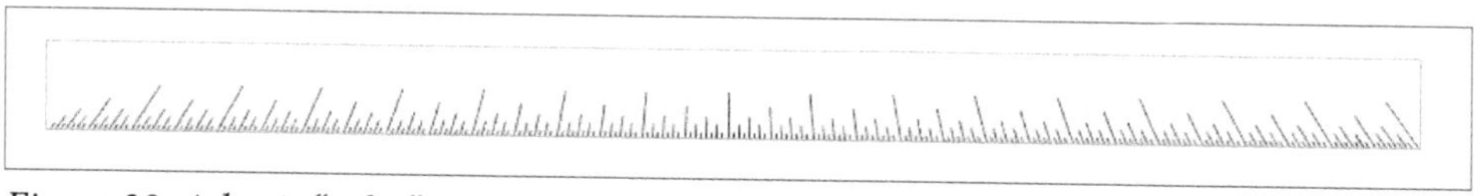

Figure 29. A basic "ruler"

What we have is a repeated background image of tick-marks on a ruler, with the `div` that contains them tiled away from us by 60 degrees. All the lines point at a common vanishing point, the top center of the container `div` (because of the `50% 0%` value for `perspective-origin`).

Now consider that same setup with various perspective origins, as shown in Figure 30.

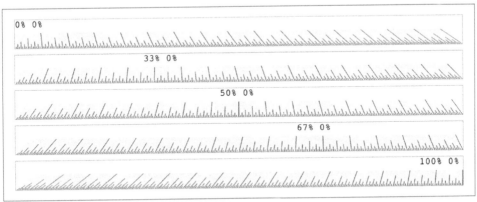

Figure 30. A basic "ruler" with different perspective origins

As you can see, moving the perspective origin changes the rendering of the 3D-transformed element.

Note that these only had an effect because we supplied a value for `perspective`. If the value of `perspective` is ever the default `none`, then any value given for `perspective-origin` will be ignored. That makes sense, since you can't have a perspective origin when there's no perspective at all!

Dealing with Backfaces

Something you probably never really thought about, over all the years you've been laying out elements, was: what would it look like if I could see the back side of the element? Now that 3D transforms are a possibility, there may well come a day when you *do* see the back side of an element. You might even mean to do so intentionally. What happens at that moment is determined by the property `backface-visibility`.

backface-visibility

Values: `visible | hidden`

Initial value: `visible`

Applies to: Any transformable element

Inherited: No

Computed value: As specified

Unlike many of the other properties and functions we've already talked about, this one is as straightforward as straightforward can be. All it does is determine whether the back side of an element is rendered when it's facing toward the viewer, or not. It really is just that simple.

So let's say you flip over two elements, one with `backface-visibility` set to the default value of `visible` and the other set to `hidden`. You get the result shown in Figure 31:

```
span {border: 1px solid red; display: inline-block;}
img {vertical-align: bottom;}
img.flip {transform: rotateX(180deg); display: inline-block;}
img#show {backface-visibility: visible;}
img#hide {backface-visibility: hidden;}

<span><img src="salmon.gif"></span>
<span><img src="salmon.gif" class="flip" id="show"></span>
<span><img src="salmon.gif" class="flip" id="hide"></span>
```

Figure 31. Visible and hidden backfaces

As you can see, the first image is unchanged. The second is flipped over around its x-axis, so we see it from the back. The third has also been flipped, but we can't see it at all because its backface has been hidden.

This property can come in handy in a number of situations. The simplest is a case where you have two elements that represent the two sides of a UI element that flips over; say, a search area with preference settings on its back, or a photo with some information on the back. Let's take the latter case. The CSS and markup might look something like this:

```
section {position: relative;}
img, div {position: absolute; top: 0; left: 0; backface-visibility: hidden;}
div {transform: rotateY(180deg);}
section:hover {transform: rotateY(180deg); transform-style: preserve-3d;}

<section>
    <img src="photo.jpg" alt="">
    <div class="info">(…info goes here…)</div>
</section>
```

Actually, this example shows that using backface-visibility isn't *quite* as simple as it first appears. It's not that the property itself is complicated, but if you forget to set transform-style to preserve-3d, then it won't work as intended. That's why transform-style is set on the section element.

There's a variant of this example that uses the same markup, but a slightly different CSS to show the image's backface when it's flipped over. This is probably more what was intended, since it makes information look like it's literally written on the back of the image. It leads to the end result shown in Figure 32:

```
section {position: relative;}
img, div {position: absolute; top: 0; left: 0;}
div {transform: rotateY(180deg); backface-visibility: hidden;
    background: rgba(255,255,255,0.85);}
section:hover {transform: rotateY(180deg); transform-style: preserve-3d;}
```

CSS: The Definitive Guide, 4th Edition

Visual Presentation for the Web

Eric A. Meyer, Estelle Weyl

O'Reilly Media, 2016

Figure 32. Photo on the front, information on the back

The only thing we had to do to make that happen was to just shift the `backface-visibilty: hidden` to the `div` instead of applying it to both the `img` and the `div`. Thus, the `div`'s backface is hidden when it's flipped over, but that of the image is not.

Summary

With the ability to transform elements in two- and three-dimensional space, CSS transforms provide a great deal of power to designers who are looking for new ways to present information. From creating interesting combinations of 2D transforms, to creating a fully 3D-acting interface, transforms open up a great deal of new territory in the design space. There are some interesting dependencies between properties, which is something that not every CSS author will find natural at first, but they become second nature with just a bit of practice.

About the Author

Eric A. Meyer has been working with the Web since late 1993 and is an internationally recognized expert on the subjects of HTML, CSS, and web standards. A widely read author, he is also the founder of Complex Spiral Consulting (*http://www.complex spiral.com*), which counts among its clients America Online; Apple Computer, Inc.; Wells Fargo Bank; and Macromedia, which described Eric as "a critical partner in our efforts to transform Macromedia Dreamweaver MX 2004 into a revolutionary tool for CSS-based design."

Beginning in early 1994, Eric was the visual designer and campus web coordinator for the Case Western Reserve University website, where he also authored a widely acclaimed series of three HTML tutorials and was project coordinator for the online version of the *Encyclopedia of Cleveland History* and the *Dictionary of Cleveland Biography*, the first encyclopedia of urban history published fully and freely on the Web.

Author of *Eric Meyer on CSS* and *More Eric Meyer on CSS* (New Riders), *CSS: The Definitive Guide* (*http://bit.ly/css-tdg-3e*) (O'Reilly), and *CSS2.0 Programmer's Reference* (Osborne/McGraw-Hill), as well as numerous articles for the O'Reilly Network, Web Techniques, and Web Review, Eric also created the CSS Browser Compatibility Charts and coordinated the authoring and creation of the W3C's official CSS Test Suite. He has lectured to a wide variety of organizations, including Los Alamos National Laboratory, the New York Public Library, Cornell University, and the University of Northern Iowa. Eric has also delivered addresses and technical presentations at numerous conferences, among them An Event Apart (which he cofounded), the IW3C2 WWW series, Web Design World, CMP, SXSW, the User Interface conference series, and The Other Dreamweaver Conference.

In his personal time, Eric acts as list chaperone of the highly active css-discuss mailing list (*http://www.css-discuss.org*), which he cofounded with John Allsopp of Western Civilisation, and which is now supported by *evolt.org*. Eric lives in Cleveland, Ohio, which is a much nicer city than you've been led to believe. For nine years he was the host of "Your Father's Oldsmobile," a big-band radio show heard weekly on WRUW 91.1 FM in Cleveland.

You can find more detailed information on Eric's personal web page (*http://www.meyerweb.com/eric*).

Colophon

The animals on the cover of *Colors, Backgrounds, and Gradients* are salmon (*salmonidae*), which is a family of fish consisting of many different species. Two of the most common salmon are the Pacific salmon and the Atlantic salmon.

Pacific salmon live in the northern Pacific Ocean off the coasts of North America and Asia. There are five subspecies of Pacific salmon, with an average weight of 10 to 30 pounds. Pacific salmon are born in the fall in freshwater stream gravel beds, where they incubate through the winter and emerge as inch-long fish. They live for a year or two in streams or lakes and then head downstream to the ocean. There they live for a few years, before heading back upstream to their exact place of birth to spawn and then die.

Atlantic salmon live in the northern Atlantic Ocean off the coasts of North America and Europe. There are many subspecies of Atlantic salmon, including the trout and the char. Their average weight is 10 to 20 pounds. The Atlantic salmon family has a life cycle similar to that of its Pacific cousins, and also travels from freshwater gravel beds to the sea. A major difference between the two, however, is that the Atlantic salmon does not die after spawning; it can return to the ocean and then return to the stream to spawn again, usually two or three times.

Salmon, in general, are graceful, silver-colored fish with spots on their backs and fins. Their diet consists of plankton, insect larvae, shrimp, and smaller fish. Their unusually keen sense of smell is thought to help them navigate from the ocean back to the exact spot of their birth, upstream past many obstacles. Some species of salmon remain landlocked, living their entire lives in freshwater.

Salmon are an important part of the ecosystem, as their decaying bodies provide fertilizer for streambeds. Their numbers have been dwindling over the years, however. Factors in the declining salmon population include habitat destruction, fishing, dams that block spawning paths, acid rain, droughts, floods, and pollution.

The cover image is a 19th-century engraving from the Dover Pictorial Archive. The cover fonts are URW Typewriter and Guardian Sans. The text font is Adobe Minion Pro; the heading font is Adobe Myriad Condensed; and the code font is Dalton Maag's Ubuntu Mono.

Get even more for your money.

Join the O'Reilly Community, and register the O'Reilly books you own. It's free, and you'll get:

- $4.99 ebook upgrade offer
- 40% upgrade offer on O'Reilly print books
- Membership discounts on books and events
- Free lifetime updates to ebooks and videos
- Multiple ebook formats, DRM FREE
- Participation in the O'Reilly community
- Newsletters
- Account management
- 100% Satisfaction Guarantee

Signing up is easy:

1. Go to: oreilly.com/go/register
2. Create an O'Reilly login.
3. Provide your address.
4. Register your books.

Note: English-language books only

To order books online:
oreilly.com/store

For questions about products or an order:
orders@oreilly.com

To sign up to get topic-specific email announcements and/or news about upcoming books, conferences, special offers, and new technologies:
elists@oreilly.com

For technical questions about book content:
booktech@oreilly.com

To submit new book proposals to our editors:
proposals@oreilly.com

O'Reilly books are available in multiple DRM-free ebook formats. For more information:
oreilly.com/ebooks